Really WILD
SHARKS

Claire Robinson

www.raintreepublishers.co.uk
Visit our website to find out more information about Raintree books.

To order:
☎ Phone 0845 6044371
🖷 Fax +44 (0) 1865 312263
✉ Email myorders@raintreepublishers.co.uk

Customers from outside the UK please telephone +44 1865 312262

Raintree is an imprint of Capstone Global Library Limited, a company incorporated in England and Wales having its registered office at 7 Pilgrim Street, London, EC4V 6LB – Registered company number: 6695582

Text © Capstone Global Library Limited 2000
The moral rights of the proprietor have been asserted.

All rights reserved. No part of this publication may be reproduced in any form or by any means (including photocopying or storing it in any medium by electronic means and whether or not transiently or incidentally to some other use of this publication) without the written permission of the copyright owner, except in accordance with the provisions of the Copyright, Designs and Patents Act 1988 or under the terms of a licence issued by the Copyright Licensing Agency, Saffron House, 6–10 Kirby Street, London EC1N 8TS (www.cla.co.uk). Applications for the copyright owner's written permission should be addressed to the publisher.

Designed by Celia Floyd
Illustrations by Alan Fraser (Pennant Illustration)
Printed and bound in China

ISBN 978 1 406 25189 0 (paperback)
16 15 14
22 21

British Library Cataloguing in Publication Data

Robinson, Claire
Shark. – (Really wild)
1. Sharks – Juvenile literature
I. Title

A full catalogue record of this book is available from the British Library

Look at the shark at the bottom of each page. Flick the pages and see what happens!

Acknowledgements
The Publishers would like to thank the following for permission to reproduce photographs: Ardea London Ltd: p.16, Valerie Taylor pp.6, 20, Ian Gordon p.19; BBC Natural History Unit: David Hall, pp.4 (right), 9, Dan Burton p.5 (left), Jeff Rotman pp.11, 21; Bruce Coleman Limited: Franco Banfi p.4 (left), Michael Glover p.18; Oxford Scientific Films: Tom McHugh p.5 (left), G.I. Bernard p.17, David B. Fleetham pp. 7, 14, 23, Bruce Watkins p.10, Richard Herrmann p.12, John Lidington p.13, Pam & Willy Kemp p.15, Tui de Roy p.22; Wildlife Matters: p.8.

Cover photograph: NHPA/A.N.T

Every effort has been made to contact copyright holders of any material reproduced in this book. Any omissions will be rectified in subsequent printings if notice is given to the publisher.

Contents

Shark relatives 4
Where do sharks live? 6
Moving around.....................8
Senses 10
Finding food 12
Feeding.................................14
Babies...................................16
Unusual sharks....................18
Sharks and people...............20
Shark facts...........................22
Glossary................................24
Index 24

Some words are shown in bold, **like this**. You can find out what they mean by looking in the glossary.

Shark relatives

Sharks are fish. The whale shark is the biggest fish in the world. Some whale sharks are 12 metres (40 feet) long.

whale shark

blue shark

black-tip reef shark

dogfish shark

Dogfish sharks are small, some are only 30 cm long. There are more than 350 different kinds of shark in the world. Let's find out how some of them live.

Where do sharks live?

Sharks are found in seas all over the world. This reef shark lives near **coral** reefs in warm, **shallow** seas. It hunts at night.

Other sharks live in deep oceans. Blue sharks and white-tip sharks are found in the Pacific, Indian and Atlantic Oceans. How many white-tip sharks can you see?

Moving around

Sharks swim by sweeping their tails from side to side. The large side fins help them to swim upwards or dive down deep.

Fish can breathe under water. They breathe in through their mouth and out through their **gills**. This shark has five gills on each side of his body.

Senses

We have eyelids to keep our eyes moist. Because sharks live under water they don't need eyelids, so you will never see a shark blink.

Sharks have good eyesight and a very strong sense of smell. This blue shark can smell something to eat a long way away. She is hungry so she goes to find food.

Finding food

Sharks are hunters. They eat other fish, octopus, and crabs. Bigger sharks eat turtles, dolphins, and sea-lions. This blue shark has found a **shoal** of fish to eat.

Some sharks find their food on the sea bed. Nurse sharks are lazy hunters. They catch slow-moving animals in **shallow** water.

Feeding

This sand shark looks very fierce. It has many rows of sharp, pointed teeth. When the front ones break off, the teeth behind move forwards to take their place.

These reef sharks smelt food and rushed in to feed. Sharks have good hearing. They can hear the sound of a fish moving quickly or struggling on a fishing line.

Babies

Some sharks give birth to live young and others lay eggs. Baby dogfish sharks grow inside an egg case called a **'mermaid's purse'**.

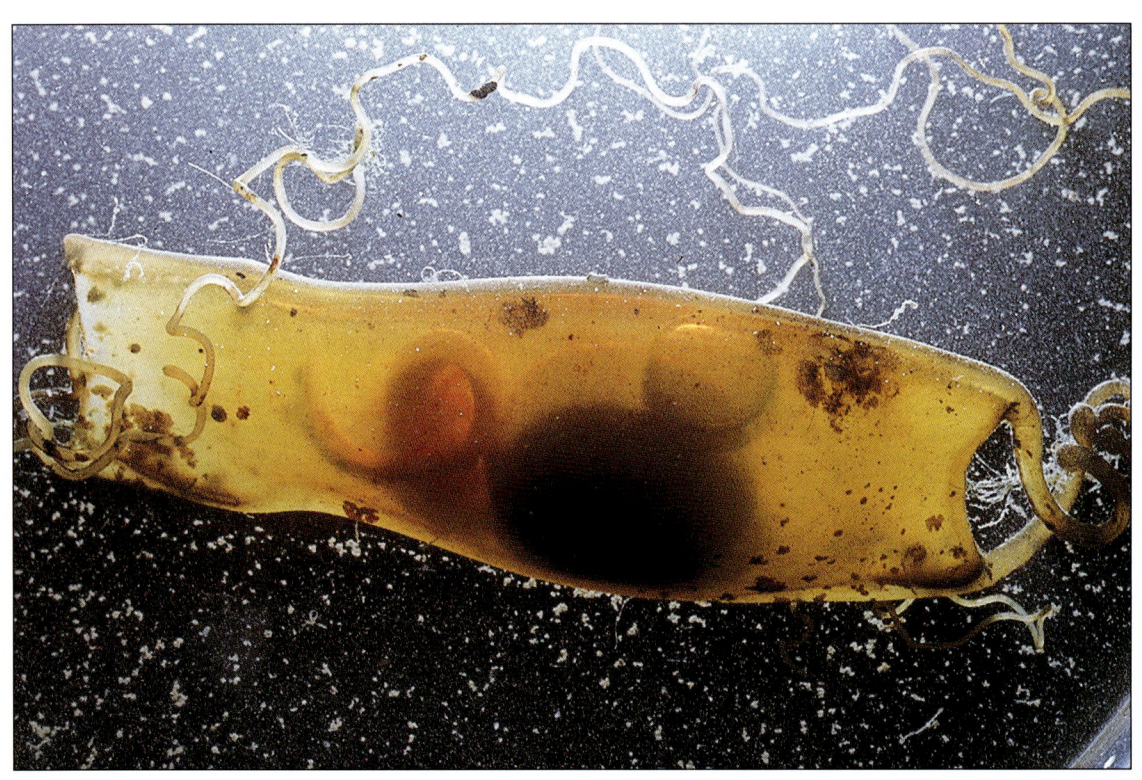

Baby sharks are called **pups**. This dogfish shark pup has just hatched from his egg case. Young sharks learn to stay together and away from adults who may eat them.

Unusual sharks

This basking shark may look fierce, but it is a gentle giant. It swims slowly near the **surface** of the water with its mouth wide open. It eats **plankton**.

Wobbegongs live near Australia. They lie very still on the sea bed waiting for octopus and crabs to pass by. The spotted pattern helps them to hide.

Sharks and people

Some sharks are in danger. Basking sharks are hunted for their oily livers. People like eating the fins and meat of black-tip sharks. Like the great white shark, these sharks are becoming **rare**.

Many people are frightened of sharks, but some people enjoy watching them and filming them. Of course, they have to be careful not to get bitten.

Shark facts

- Most sharks are less than 2 metres (6 feet) long. The smallest shark is only 25 cm (10 inches) long.

- A shark's skeleton is not made of bone, but **gristle**, rather like the tip of your nose.

- A hammerhead shark is named after the shape of its head.

- Sharks have between two and over 100 **pups**. Pregnant females have their babies away from other sharks and where there is plenty of food.

- In some parts of the world, swimmers have been attacked by sharks. The great white shark is one of the most dangerous. But far more people are killed by cars than by sharks.

Glossary

coral a hard ridge made by millions of tiny sea animals

gills the slits at the side of a fish's head, used for breathing

gristle a strong material that makes up a shark's skeleton

mermaid's purse the egg case of a dogfish

plankton tiny plants and animals in the sea

pup a baby shark

rare not many left

shallow not deep

shoal a big group of fish

surface the top of something, in this case the sea

Index

babies   16, 17, 23, 24
breathing   9, 24
eyes   10, 11
food   12, 15, 18, 19, 23
hearing   15
hunting   6, 11, 12, 13, 18, 19, 20
smelling   11, 15
swimming   8, 18
teeth   14